# THE IMPORTANCE OF THE

# Columbia & Rio Grande

## RIVERS

American Geography Grade 5 |
Children's Geography & Cultures Books

**BABY PROFESSOR**
EDUCATION KIDS

First Edition, 2020

Published in the United States by Speedy Publishing LLC, 40 E Main Street, Newark, Delaware 19711 USA.

© 2020 Baby Professor Books, an imprint of Speedy Publishing LLC

Baby Professor Books are available at special discounts when purchased in bulk for industrial and sales-promotional use. For details contact our Special Sales Team at Speedy Publishing LLC, 40 E Main Street, Newark, Delaware 19711 USA. Telephone (888) 248-4521 Fax: (210) 519-4043.

10 9 8 7 6 * 5 4 3 2 1

Print Edition: 9781541960817
Digital Edition: 9781541963818

*See the world in pictures. Build your knowledge in style.*
*www.speedypublishing.com*

# TABLE OF CONTENTS

Rivers are only one of the many sources of water on Earth.

Did you know that there is more water on the Earth than there is land? In fact, water makes up a little more than seventy percent of the surface of the Earth. Water is also a very powerful force on Earth. There are many different sources of water. This book will talk about one source: rivers. The book will provide a basic definition of what a river is and then the rest of the book will talk about how two great rivers in the United States, The Columbia River and the Rio Grande, have proven to be very important.

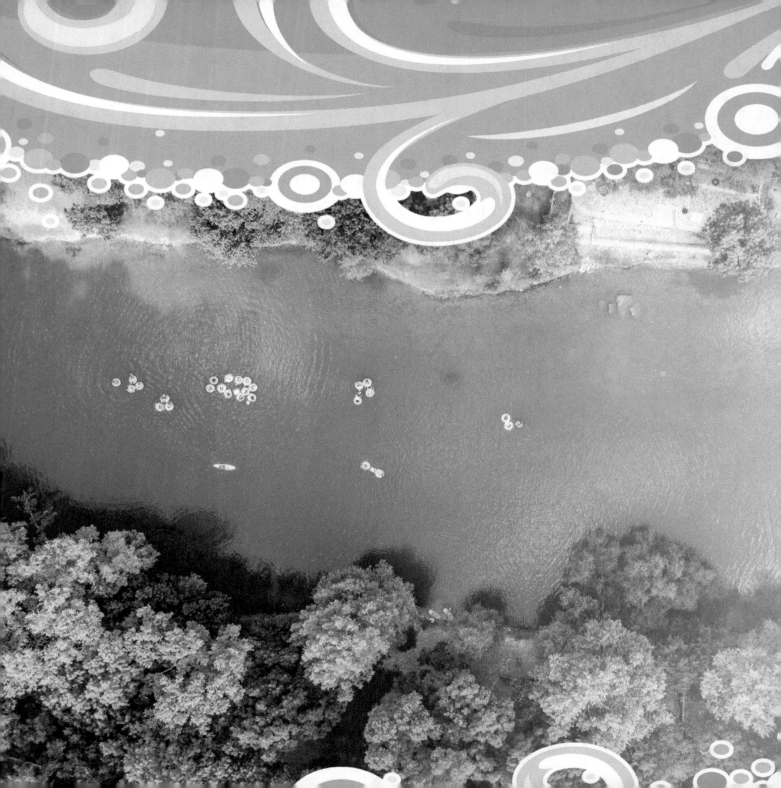

# A Basic Definition of What a River is

River flowing in the forest

A river can be defined as a source of water which naturally flows along a specific path over land.

It can start with a very small source or a trickle. It starts to travel downhill and along its route, other trickles or streams of water get added to it. After a while, a lot of water has joined the flow until what is formed is called a river.

A river can start with a very small trickle and travel downhill.

As the river gains speed, it picks up both soil and gravel along its path.

After the flow of water has formed into a river, it gains speed. Both soil and gravel are picked up and join the waterflow.

Along the way, water from streams join the river. A tributary is the name given to a stream which joins a river. The river continues to move and the tributaries are referred to as a river system.

Aerial view of a large river and smaller tributary rivers

A river mouth is the part where the river joins a larger body of water like the sea or ocean.

A river eventually reaches its mouth, which is the part where the river joins the sea or an ocean and its water flows into that sea or ocean. Naturally, the water flows downwards due to gravity which is why sea level is often considered the baseline to measure height for geographical formations.

While in everyday language, people often use the terms river and stream interchangeably, there are some critical differences between the two. A river is much deeper and larger than a stream thus containing a greater volume of water.

You can walk across a stream but not across a river.

It is generally understood that a person could cross a stream by foot but would not be able to ford a river. Another difference is that a stream is simply one independent flowing body of water. However, a river has many streams that feed into it which is part of what makes it bigger and deeper than a mere stream.

# The Columbia River

The Columbia River is a very important river in the northwestern part of the United States. The main source of the river is Columbia Lake which is located not too far from the Rocky Mountains in British Columbia, Canada.

Columbia Lake with Canadian Rockies in the background in British Columbia, Canada

Columbia River, Washington

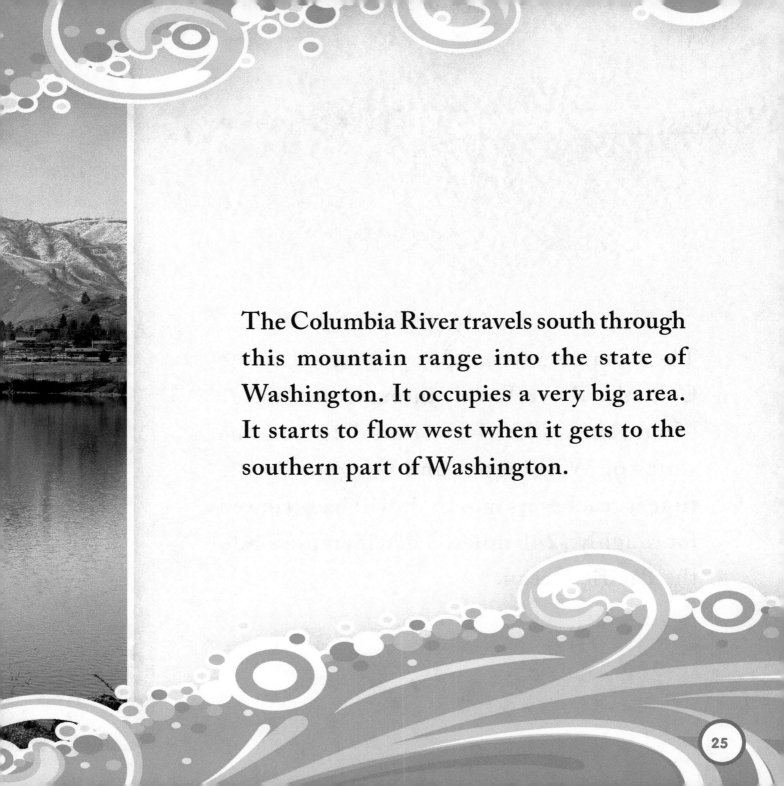

The Columbia River travels south through this mountain range into the state of Washington. It occupies a very big area. It starts to flow west when it gets to the southern part of Washington.

The Columbia River Gorge is fomed by the Columbia River flowing through the Cascade Mountains. The river flows between the states of Washington and Oregon. By the time it reaches its mouth, it will have flowed for roughly 1240 miles. Then it empties into the Pacific Ocean.

Columbia River Gorge, Oregon

# The Importance of the Columbia River to the Economy

T he Columbia River has an abundance of marine life. One part of the river in particular, a very big estuary, the area of a river that is influenced by ocean tides, boasts many different types of marine life.

The Columbia River estuary

A large school of salmon

One type of fish that contributes to the economy in the northwest is salmon. Many salmon are caught and sold and this brings in revenue. Sadly, there has been a reduction in the number of salmon. There used to be a lot more.

Bonneville Dam on the Columbia River
between Oregon and Washington

Another way in which the Columbia River is important is that it is a source of hydroelectric energy, which is also known by the terms hydroelectric power and hydroelectricity. Many dams have been erected at different points on the Columbia River. The dams help with hydroelectric energy. A lot of energy is available from water right before it passes over a dam. The energy from the force of the water is used to produce electricity. This electricity is then made available for use through a power plant. Each power plant customer can receive the electricity for their everyday needs.

Because the Columbia River has so many different dams, it has been given the nickname Electric River. Of all the hydroelectric energy produced in the United States, approximately one third comes from the dams along the Columbia River.

The Dalles Dam on the Columbia River in Oregon

Rain near the mouth of the Columbia River helps in maintaining the evergreen forest in the area.

The Columbia River is important because it influences the physical environment around it. A lot of precipitation in the form of rain is common near the mouth of the Columbia River. The rain is of great benefit in maintaining the evergreen forest in the area.

Other parts of the river, such as near the source, are drier. This helps different types of trees to flourish. Examples include fir, pine and larch.

Different types of trees thrive near the source of the Columbia River.

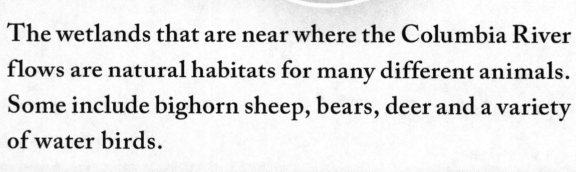

The wetlands that are near where the Columbia River flows are natural habitats for many different animals. Some include bighorn sheep, bears, deer and a variety of water birds.

Bighorn sheep grazing above the Columbia River Valley. British Columbia.

Caspian Terns flying above the Columbia River surface.

The Columbia River is also important because it is used for personal reasons by many households along its path. This includes being used as a source of drinking water for many people.

The Columbia River is used as a source of drinking water for many people.

In addition, it is used as irrigation for a lot of farmland that is near the river. For food to be produced, the land on which it is grown must be irrigated. Because the Columbia River covers such a long stretch of the northwest region of the United States, it is used for irrigation purposes for many farms.

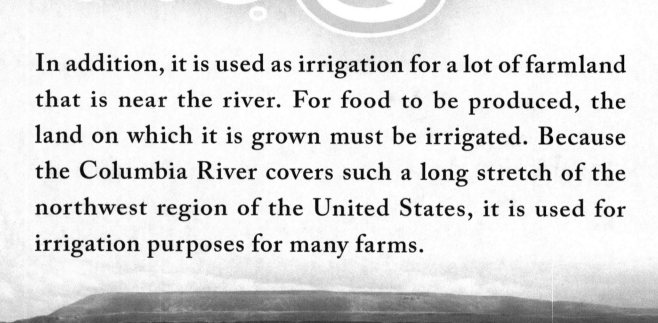

An abundance of food is grown in the Columbia River Basin.

Pumping station on the Columbia River to provide water for irrigation.

# The Rio Grande

The Rio Grande, which is Spanish for Great River, is a very long river. It is also known as Río Grande del Norte, which is Spanish for "big river of the north". It is the fifth longest river on the continent of North America. Its source is in the San Juan Mountains which are in the southwest region of the state of Colorado.

Island Lake in the San Juan Mountains near Silverton, Colorado

Rio Grande River near Abiquiu, New Mexico

The Rio Grande travels southeast and passes through the states of New Mexico and Texas. By the time it reaches its mouth, which is the Gulf of Mexico, it will have traveled 1900 miles. Most of the river, 1300 miles, stretches between the state of Texas and the country of Mexico. The Rio Grande is called by a different name in Mexico. It is Río Bravo del Norte, which in English means "wild river of the north."

# The Importance of the Rio Grande

The Rio Grande is important for economic reasons. It generates money from both trade and tourism. Two cities, Laredo and El Paso, both in the state of Texas, are port cities. Port cities allow for the trading of goods to flow from one place to another. If a country has port cities, it will have a way to make money from the flow of goods that take place in a port.

Downtown city skyline of El Paso, Texas

Shops on Hidalgo Street in downtown Laredo, Texas

In addition to revenue gathered from trade, a port city is also an entry point for tourists. When tourists arrive in a city, the local economy benefits from the money that they bring in and spend at places such as restaurants, hotels and shops.

Reservoirs along the Rio Grande are very popular areas for recreation and outdoor adventure. People enjoy fishing, boating, and swimming. Naturally, these activities bring in revenue for local businesses.

Reservoirs along the Rio Grande are very popular areas for recreation and outdoor adventure.

The Rio Grande flows for around 107 miles along the boundary of Big Bend National Park in southwest Texas. It is a beautiful area which attracts a lot of tourists.

Rio Grande and Big Bend National Park in Texas, border of U.S. and Mexico

The Rio Grande is important for providing both electricity and irrigation. There are many dams on the Rio Grande, with most of them being in New Mexico. The dams help to channel water for irrigation and they also serve as a source of hydroelectric power. As a source of hydroelectricity, the Rio Grande is very important to those who rely on it for power.

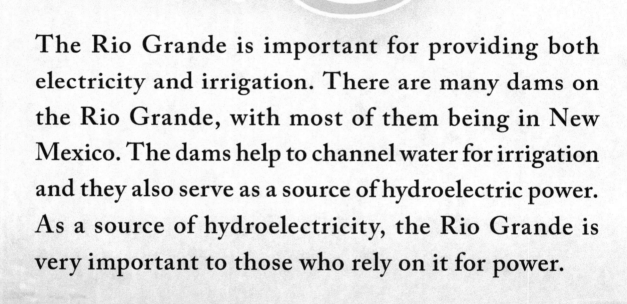

Elephant Butte Dam on the Rio Grande near Truth or Consequences, New Mexico

Falcon Power Plant dam on the Rio Grande between Texas and Mexico

FALCON POWER PLANT
UNITED STATES UNIT

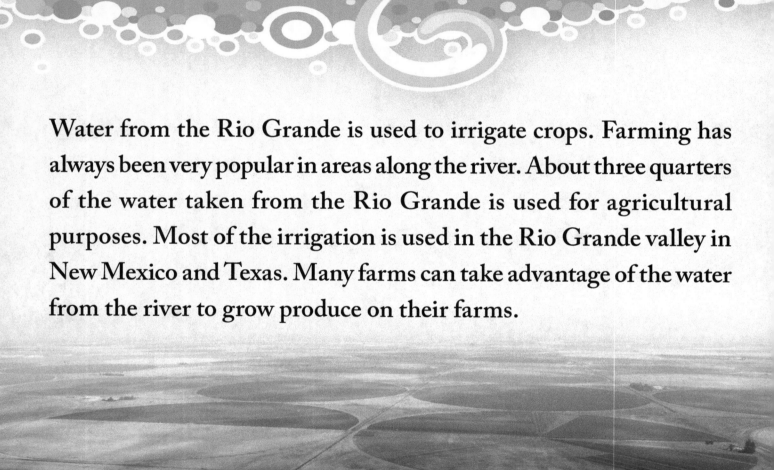

Water from the Rio Grande is used to irrigate crops. Farming has always been very popular in areas along the river. About three quarters of the water taken from the Rio Grande is used for agricultural purposes. Most of the irrigation is used in the Rio Grande valley in New Mexico and Texas. Many farms can take advantage of the water from the river to grow produce on their farms.

Circular fields in the Rio Grande Valley

Not only is the Rio Grande important because it provides water for irrigation, it also helps the economy. Because food can be grown, it is able to be sold for profit.

Irrigation Canal in Rio Grande Valley of Texas

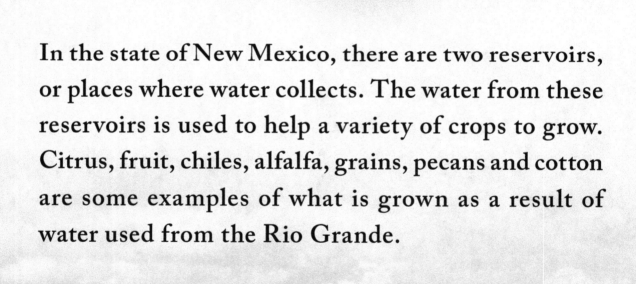

In the state of New Mexico, there are two reservoirs, or places where water collects. The water from these reservoirs is used to help a variety of crops to grow. Citrus, fruit, chiles, alfalfa, grains, pecans and cotton are some examples of what is grown as a result of water used from the Rio Grande.

Rows of crops along the Rio Grande in far-south Texas.

The Rio Grande is also used as a source of drinking water for very many people.

Drinking water sourced from the Rio Grande.

The Rio Grande helps to sustain life in nature. Areas surrounding the source of the river benefit from the cool and humid effects brought on by the waterflow. The growth of trees such as fir, aspen and spruce flourish in this type of environment.

The Rio Grande helps to sustain life in nature.

Even in the southern areas where the river flows, growth is present. However, the type of growth is quite different. Plants that can survive dessert conditions, such as different types of cacti, for example, grow there.

Prickly Pear Cactus and Ocotillo grow in the southern areas of Rio Grande

The location of the Rio Grande had a significant role with becoming a natural border between the United States and Mexico. The United States and Mexico had an armed conflict between 1846 and 1848. It was called The Mexican War, which is also known as The Mexican-American War. In Mexico, it was given the name Intervención Estadounidense en México, which in English means United States Intervention in Mexico.

U.S. forces attacking Monterey, Mexico during the Mexican-American War in 1846.

Cover of the exchange copy of the treaty of Guadalupe Hidalgo

In 1848, both the United States and Mexico signed an agreement. In the agreement, it was officially decided that the Rio Grande would serve as the border between the two countries.

Both the Columbia River and the Rio Grande play important roles in the United States. These two rivers are important because they help with the economy and with nature.

Columbia River

There is a lot of reliance on the rivers, for the maintenance of nature, for personal use and for industrial use.

Rio Grande

Unfortunately, there have been some problems with the rivers in recent years. Some of these problems include too much water being used, pollution and a reduction in marine life. It is important to take a close look at these problems so that the water can continue to be harnessed but respected so that the rivers will be of benefit for many years to come. With all the uses of these two rivers, their importance cannot be underestimated. Therefore, it is crucial that the rivers do not run dry and do not become so polluted so that they can no longer sustain wildlife.

*Visit*

## www.speedypublishing.com

To view and download free content
on your favorite subject and browse
our catalog of new and exciting
books for readers of all ages.

Printed in the USA
CPSIA information can be obtained
at www.ICGtesting.com
LVHW050256280923
759263LV00007B/572

9 781541 979666